W9-AZJ-902

Beautiful
Georgia

Beautiful
Georgia

Text by Paul M. Lewis

Library of Congress Cataloging in Publication Data
Lewis, Paul M.
  Beautiful Georgia
    1. Georgia—Description and travel—1951-
I. Title.
F291.2.L48   975.8   78-7895
ISBN 0-915796-42-2
ISBN 0-915796-41-4 (paperback)

First Printing October 1978

Published by Beautiful America Publishing Company
4720 S.W. Washington, Beaverton, Oregon 97005
Robert D. Shangle, Publisher

PHOTO CREDITS

WILLIAM J. ALLEN—*page 18, below.*

S. ANDERSON—*page 54, below.*

BURFORD BURCH—*page 40, below; pages 48-49.*

BOB BUSBY—*page 11, below; pages 12-13.*

ED COOPER—*pages 44-45; page 50, below; page 52.*

JOHN M. HALL—*page 10; page 46, above; page 69; page 72.*

SHEL HALL—*page 19; page 68.*

TOM JONES—*page 21, above; page 55.*

RICHARD LUBRANT—*page 9; page 28, below; page 42; page 47; page 56.*

CHUCK ROGERS—*page 20.*

ROBERT SHANGLE—*page 11, above; page 18, above; page 23; page 43, above; page 53, above; page 57; page 60, below; page 65, above.*

KEVIN SHULER—*page 14, below; page 28, above.*

STATE OF GEORGIA, TOURISM DIVISION—*page 21, below; page 22, below; page 25, above; page 25, below; page 32; page 36, above; page 36, below; page 41; page 46, below; page 50, above; page 51; page 60, above; page 61; page 64; page 65, below.*

AL STEPHENSON—*page 14, above; page 22, above; page 33, above; page 40, above.*

PETER H. STEWART—*page 24; page 29.*

TOMMY THOMPSON—*page 33, below.*

MARK WILLIAMS—*page 15; pages 16-17.*

DEAN WOHLGEMUTH—*page 43, below; page 53, below.*

ARCHER M. YATES—*page 54, above.*

Enlarged Prints

CONTENTS

Beautiful America Publishing Company

The nation's foremost publisher of quality color photography.

CURRENT BOOKS

Utah, Texas, Alaska, Hawaii, Georgia, Arizona, Montana, Michigan, Colorado, Washington, Minnesota, California, California II, No. California, No. California II, So. California, San Francisco, Oregon II, British Columbia, California Missions, Western Impressions, Lewis & Clark Country.

FORTHCOMING BOOKS IN 1979

Massachusetts, Pennsylvania, Maryland, Wisconsin, Kentucky, Florida, Illinois, Ohio, Idaho, North Idaho, California Coast, Oregon Mountains, Nevada, New Mexico, Montana II, Rocky Mountains, North Carolina, South Carolina, Virginia, Oklahoma, Michigan II, Mississippi, Kentucky, Missouri.

1979 CALENDARS

Hawaii, Oregon, Colorado, California, Michigan, Washington, Western America, Beautiful America.

Send for complete catalog, 50 ᶜ
Beautiful America Publishing Company
4720 S.W. Washington
Beaverton, Oregon 97005

INTRODUCTION

Georgia is a state that people keep hearing about these days. It does a lot for a state's image when a native son becomes President of the United States.

But what the rest of the country is just finding out, native Georgians have known all along: there's a lot to see in this state. For starters, its borders take in more square miles than any other state east of the Mississippi, embracing a great variety of terrain, from coastal plains and swamps to rolling hills to mountains. And it has history, with many monuments to its past carefully preserved and proudly displayed around the state.

There is so much to Georgia that it would take many volumes of color photographs to do it justice. Such is not the aim of the present book. It is supposed to be a tribute to and a celebration of one of the beautiful places in this country, nothing more. We hope the exquisite color portraits that follow will convey a sense of Georgia's unique charms: the wilderness beauty of the Golden Isles and Okefenokee, or the cultivated ambience of human efforts in Callaway Gardens or antebellum Savannah.

The text is not a tour of Georgia, just as the photographs do no more than sample the physical reality. I have discussed only a few of the state's interesting places and aspects; the omission of others does not indicate any notion of mine about their worthiness. I hope I have managed to say enough to give the reader the conviction that here is a beautiful and liveable place that is taking pains to stay that way.

Georgians are as prideful as any who know that their part of the world is special, but they don't use the hard sell to convince visitors of that reality. They don't need to. The good taste bred by a long tradition of hospitality allows them to let their environment—natural and man-made—speak for itself. That it does, and eloquently.

The love of natural beauty is strong in Georgia and so is the preservationist ethos. That sense of values and of tradition has brought the state into the last quarter of the 20th century with significant parts of it as wild and beautiful as they were before the first settlers. The state of the state of Georgia in these times of deteriorating environments is very good, and continuing close concern by Georgians holds the promise of continued good health for their beautiful Eden.

P.M.L.

6

THE GOLDEN ISLES

The Spanish settlers of the 1500s called some of them the Golden Isles of Guale. Guale was the Indian chief who received the first soldiers who landed on St. Catherines, the first island to be settled by the Spanish. Nowadays, "The Golden Isles" means all fifteen of Georgia's Barrier Islands, those last remaining strips of sand, grass, and forests in the East Coast chain of islands that are still, more or less, wild and free.

The Barrier Islands stretch along Georgia's coastline with hardly a break. This rich endowment has provided the state with an ecological and commercial treasure beyond reckoning. By protecting the waters on the mainland side, they have allowed the establishment of tidal salt marshes where plant life per acre can be ten times the yield of a comparable field of crops on the mainland.

Aside from their productivity, these islands are an exceptional gift of nature for their own sake. Some people think they are just about the loveliest parcels of wilderness in the whole offshore chain. One would not want to argue the point. Where nature has been allowed to maintain her systems, unhindered by artificial installations and improvements, the distinctive wilderness environments prevail. These islands have indeed remained the closest approach to paradise available to earth-bound beings.

The three "developed" islands are St. Simons, Sea Island, and Jeckyll. Because they are connected to the mainland by causeways they are readily accessible to the auto tourist. Development has removed them from the list of wild and free places. Still, while the islands have been tamed, they have not been destroyed. Resort orientation has tended to take advantage of the stunning natural setting, producing an environment of extraordinary appeal.

The incredible part of the story is that so many of the Golden Isles have remained truly golden, unspoiled by the rapid pace of technological civilization that has proceeded on the mainland so close to them. North to south the islands are: Wassaw, Ossabaw, St. Catherines, Blackbeard, Sapelo, Wolf, and what may be the greatest prize of them all—Cumberland. Their primitive condition is largely a matter of early luck and latter-day concern. Parts of them have long been in the hands of wealthy families whose main interest has been in seeing them preserved as they are.

Some are now parts of the National Wildlife Refuge system. Wassaw, Wolf, and Blackbeard are in this category. Some others are under state jurisdiction, including Ossabaw, one of the biggest (43 square miles) and wildest. The biggest and wildest of all is Cumberland, near the Georgia-Florida border. Now most of it is owned by the National Park Service; it was designated as the Cumberland Island National Seashore in 1972. The Park Service regards it as one of the most pristine seashores remaining on the Atlantic and Gulf coasts.

A member of the Carnegie family, which owned most of Cumberland at one time, has helped keep it that way. Mrs. Lucy Ferguson, granddaughter of Thomas and Lucy Carnegie, still owns one of the three major private holdings on the island. She has long been a leader in the struggle to preserve Cumberland in its wild state. And when the Park Service eventually acquires the whole island it is mandated to do just that—preserve. Other national seashores have emphasized recreation and have been developed with that as the ruling consideration. But the intent of Congress for Cumberland is clear—the island must be preserved as nearly as possible in its primitive state. The Park Service has been drawing up plans to carry out this intent, including limited access for visitors, and limited facilities for those visitors.

The Golden Isles, at their wildest, know no civilization. Cumberland has long, long stretches of wide, white hard sand beaches on its eastern shores; vast salt marshes on its western side that nourish plant and aquatic life; and, in the middle, great forests of moss-draped live oaks. Just as the marshes are home to a rich variety of aquatic life, the forests provide shelter for a large assortment of animals, including deer, otter, raccoon, wild pig, and various rodents. The long, wide beaches have made Cumberland an important rookery for the Atlantic loggerhead turtle, a species that has been on the decline in this century. The bird population is extensive, too, with wading birds in the salt marshes and freshwater pools, and shore birds such as sandpipers and terns. Migratory fowl use the island's big Lake Whitney as a stopover. Crab species are numerous in many areas of the island, as are alligators and snakes.

Georgia's Barrier Islands have a long and fascinating history of involvement in human affairs, probably beginning with the Indians thousands of years ago. Spanish soldiers and settlers arrived in the 1500s and, later on, the British claimed some of the islands. During the plantation years in the 1700s and 1800s parts of the islands were in private hands. On Cumberland and St. Simons, long-fibered cotton was grown, along with sugar cane. The islands' live oaks were heavily logged for shipbuilding, being tougher wood than the mainland variety of live oak. Thomas Spaulding, a Scotsman, bought up most of Sapelo by the middle 1800s after having become wealthy in the production of cotton and sugar cane on the southern end of the island. Blackbeard Island, across a creek from the northern end of Sapelo, was

(Preceding page) Autumn's chill touches the Appalachian Mountains with color.

(Opposite) Many varieties of plant and aquatic life may be found in and around the waters of Billy Lake, in Okefenokee.

(Right) A water lily lies on the placid waters of a Georgia pond.

(Below) A whitewater creek makes its rugged way through the forest to the valley floor.

(Following pages) The interior of Cumberland Island presents a vista virtually unaltered by the presence of man.

(Second following page, above) Deciduous forest meets pastureland at Blue Ridge.

(Below) Morning sun casts long shadows on the windward side of Jeckyll Island.

(Third following page) The Chattahoochee River moves quietly between forested banks.

(Preceding pages) Red sky in the morning—sunrise begins to lighten the blue shadows in the Cumberland Island dunes.
(Left) Brightly-colored flowering shrubs grace the grounds of Stone Mountain State Park.
(Below) Lush forest growth crowds close to the edge of the Satilla River.
(Opposite) A rugged waterfall interrupts this clear-running North Georgia stream.

(Left) Winter's bare branches are covered with snow along this North Georgia stream.

(Right) Colorful wildflowers line the fencerows in the Georgia countryside.

(Below) Crisp autumn air brings a touch of color to the tree-lined country roads.

(Following page, above) A gentle breeze ruffles the surface of this lake outside of Soches.

(Following page, below) Atlanta's burgeoning growth has made striking additions to the city's ever-changing skyline.

(Second following page) Georgia's mild climate and fertile land promotes lush growth of brush and wildflowers.

(Third following page) Cold, clear Smith Creek makes its way through the autumn-tinged Ruby Falls Recreation Area, in the Chattahoochee National Forest.

believed to have been the headquarters of that bold English pirate who carved out a colorful and terrifying career along the Georgia and Carolina coasts during the early 1700s.

Today, Wassaw Island is the only one with virgin forests remaining. But the Barriers are still mostly wilderness, despite their long history of involvement in human affairs. The Indians and the Spanish and the English changed nothing basic about the islands they settled on. Here and there are traces that bespeak their one-time presence, but exuberant natural growth has made them a part of the wild landscape again. So far, restraint has paid off by inflicting no permanent injury to these havens.

(Preceding page, above) Morning mists begin to dispel as the sun rises over Savannah.
(Preceding page, below) Hardy pines grow on some rocky Georgia foothills.

ANTEBELLUM HOMES

Antebellum means "before the war," and in the South that can only refer to the War Between the States. Homes that survived the violence of war and the economic disasters in its aftermath are accorded great honor as remnants of a vanished era.

When thinking about such structures, one is likely to picture tall, graceful columns and white-painted clapboard. Many examples of this style are indeed preserved in many localities, but this is only one of the many architectural types that were favored by wealthy merchants and planters. The Greek Revival (as it is called in the descriptive literature) was most typically represented in the dignified facade of two-story columns and fanlighted entrance doors. Some of the other styles popular during this period were Italianate, Georgian, Colonial, Federal, and combinations of these. Victorian touches were added later as embellishment to some of the earlier styles.

The Atlanta-Savannah and Atlanta-Augusta axes are exceptionally well represented by carefully preserved private homes and other structures that were built before the War Between the States. The west and west central parts of Georgia can also boast of many such buildings. Rome in the north, Newnan, Columbus, and Cuthbert have some of these elegant reminders of the early and middle 19th century, some of them well-preserved and some falling into decay.

Among the big cities—Atlanta, Savannah, Columbus, Macon and Augusta—the biggest, Atlanta, is the only one without some representation remaining of the antebellum days. Sherman's armies left very little to preserve. Savannah was spared the holocaust and today is filled with beautiful and gracious reminders of its early history. But Savannah is a whole story by itself, and a separate chapter of this commentary has been reserved for that unique part of the Georgia scene.

It is only right that Augusta, Georgia's second oldest city, be enriched by reminders of former times. It was founded by General William Oglethorpe in 1735 as

(Following page, above) The leeward side of Cumberland Island looks toward the mainland over a rich estuarine environment.

(Following page, below) This rowdy little creek is actually the headwaters of the Chattahoochee River, which begins in the hills near Helen.

a trading post and fortress town against the Cherokee Indians. It has grown with great vitality since then as an industrial power and the center of a diversified agricultural area that comprises eastern Georgia and western South Carolina. The Savannah River is Augusta's pathway to the sea, and was, during the early years of this century, a destroyer of much property with its floodwaters. But the Savannah is leashed now by the huge Clark Hill Dam upriver of the city.

Unfortunately for Augusta and for our heritage in general, a monstrous fire in 1916 accomplished to a great extent what Sherman neglected to do when he bypassed the city in 1864 on his March to the Sea. Many historic homes were destroyed in that disaster, but some fine examples remain to anchor Augusta to its colorful past. Some of these homes have been remodeled for use as public buildings, retaining their distinctive features and graceful lines. One of these is the Nicholas Ware Mansion, on Telfair Street downtown, being used now as an art school. This building is two-story frame, and is regarded as the purest example of Georgian style in the city. Among its features are horseshoe-shaped entrance steps enhanced by mahogany railings; there is a graceful winding stairway inside. The house was built in 1818 and was the scene of a ball—in 1825—for the Marquis de La Fayette.

Nearby on Green Street are three more fine houses. One, the Charles Phinizy Place, at 519, is also in the Georgian mode. Built in 1841, it has three stories over a high basement. Its facade of hand-made red brick gives it a decidedly mellow air, as does its elegant iron-railed horseshoe stairway that leads to a high entrance balcony on the second-floor level. Nearby, at 503, is a house with four fluted Doric columns supporting a classic triangular pediment. Now used as a county health headquarters, the building is lavishly adorned by delicate hand-wrought iron grillwork on the exterior and hand-carved woodwork in the interior. The third example, at 426, is known as the De L'Aigle House, a combination of Tudor design with Greek Revival columns. It was build by Nicholas De L'Aigle in 1818. Much elaborate carving is evident in many features of this house, including interior wood and brass work and the front entrance door.

More antebellum structures can be found in downtown Augusta, including churches, institutional buildings, and private homes. Further examples can be found in that part of Augusta called The Hill—the Sand Hills section. In the early days, some residents of the low-lying city built summer homes or ''cottages'' on The Hill to escape from the sweaty humidity of the river land and swamplands round about. A few of these are still in existence, dating back to the late 18th and early 19th centuries, and are still used as private homes.

(Preceding page) Leaves litter the boulder-strewn bed of the Hiawassee River, just north of Robertstown.

Columbus, the big town on the western border with Alabama, hums with traffic on its main arteries (Ft. Benning is close by on the south), but the pace is different when one gets away from these feeder roads. The streets of the old town are broad—up to 164 feet—and flanked by live oaks and other giant trees. Some of the finest old residences are on Broadway, a couple of blocks up from the Chattahoochee River, and on the next few streets to the east. Columbus is notable for its church buildings, particularly those on Church Square (a whole block so reserved when the city was founded in 1828). Two massive structures occupy this area. One, the First Baptist Church, is a Greek Revival combination of brick and lofty Doric columns. The other, St. Luke Methodist Church, is Colonial in design. Both churches date from the founding of Columbus, although the latter one has been rebuilt since that time.

Many of the smaller communities east of Atlanta have carefully preserved their heritage of elegant and dignified antebellum homes. Among these are Athens, the home of the University of Georgia; Covington; Eatonton; Warrenton; Waynesboro, and Washington. Many of the buildings in Athens, including a number identified with the university, are antebellum and announce their age in various guises. The doric column is much in evidence but also some of the softer, more gracious aspects of the early architectural tastes are there. Athens, Washington, and—southwest of Atlanta—Newnan contain houses with spacious porches, some with elaborate Victorian ornamentation centered upon supporting pillars. These porches usually extend around the front and one or two sides of the house.

The towns of Covington, Eatonton, and Milledgeville—all east-southeast of Atlanta—are like history books of deep-South architecture. Milledgeville especially shows the gradual evolution of the Grecian style from the simple front stoop into the elaborate doorway treatment and prominent porches on first and second floors. The fancy verandahs that sometimes extend around three sides of the house seem to gild the lily, but they are usually works of art in their own right.

(Following page) This striking North Georgia waterfall plunges into a tree-shaded canyon.

GEORGIA'S SCENIC RIVERS

Georgia is generously endowed with interesting rivers. Though these waterways have long been significant as transportation lanes, they have a lot going for them besides water. Long stretches are very beautiful and quite wild, and some have figured in Georgia's and the nation's history. Starting at the northeast corner of the state, the eight most important rivers are, in clockwise order: Savannah, Ogeechee, Altamaha, St. Marys, Suwanee, Flint, Chattahoochee and Coosa.

The Savannah River, forming most of the border between Georgia and South Carolina, was long ago harnessed to do man's work. Partly because of it the cities of Augusta and Savannah along its banks have become great economic powers. Savannah, near the river's mouth, is muddy, muddier than it used to be, a consequence of intensive farming operations in the areas it drains and of power projects on the upper river. It is 314 miles long, and a great deal of that length is between Augusta and Savannah where the river twists and turns in upon itself as if loath to reach the point where it must give up its waters to the sea. The course of the river carries it through the swamplands of the coastal plain, where slash pine grows in dense forests. A fast-growing tree even under adverse conditions, slash pine contributes much to the economy of Georgia because of the variety of materials that can be derived from it, including pulp and naval stores.

A very different stream flows almost parallel to the Savannah a few miles to the south. The Ogeechee extends for 250 miles from north-central Georgia to Ossabaw Sound on the coast, flanked by the Barrier Islands of Wassaw and Ossabaw. It is like a river of another time, with thickly forested banks of great beauty, in many places unmarked by civilization. But quite in keeping with the river's quiet charm are the old antebellum houses seen once in a while along its length.

The mighty and mysterious Altamaha River flows through southeast Georgia's swampland to the sea at St. Simon's Island. Not much has been done to change this river, although it has long been a highway to the sea for Macon. The Altamaha proper is only 80 air miles long, but several times that when all its wrigglings and squirmings are counted. It is a very big river because of two tributaries—the Oconee

(Preceding page, above) Springtime brings out the dogwood blossoms in Piedmont Park, Atlanta.
(Preceding page, below) By day the Atlanta skyline shows new construction that will soon change its profile.

and the Ocmulgee—which drain an extensive area in middle Georgia before they combine to form the Altamaha.

The virgin cypresses and pines along its banks have long ago been cut and floated as log rafts downriver to Darien. But other forests have grown up and still shelter a large population of wildlife, such as bear, wildcat and rattlesnake. The river itself is a rich fishing stream where sturgeon are sometimes taken weighing more than 350 pounds, bringing with them large amounts of very good caviar. Particularly in its 20-mile-long delta area, where the Altamaha winds around innumerable islands, the sea life of the river is rich almost beyond belief. This delta qualifies as one of the world's premier fishing grounds in addition to being a waterfowl reserve.

The St. Marys River delineates the eastern part of the Georgia-Florida border. This southeastern stream is very deep, very dark, and lazy. It enters the sea at the town of St. Marys after oozing indolently out of the Okefenokee and flowing along undisturbed by any commercial traffic or even by very many human visitors at all. Great stretches of lonely pine forests along its banks once sheltered pirates during the Spanish era in Florida. The river itself was a subject of strenuous arguments between France, England and Spain when those nations were fighting for control of the east coast. The only contest of any kind these days regarding the St. Marys is between Georgia and Florida, and that is merely a gentlemanly debate as to the river's source. Georgia claims the honor for Okefenokee, and Florida opts for some small streams on its side of the border.

A river that certainly does originate in Georgia is the Suwanee. It oozes from swamp springs in the Okefenokee National Wildlife Refuge, where its waters are stained a dark brown as it winds through the dense cypress stands. Stephen Foster, who never laid eyes on the Suwanee, wrote a folk melody about it that made it one of the world's most famous rivers. The Suwanee hasn't changed much, even since "Old Folks at Home" gave it so much celebrity. Its tea-colored waters still drift slowly, slowly through the big swamp in a southwesterly direction, visiting northern Florida, and finally, after 200 miles, emptying into the Gulf of Mexico.

A river with many roles is the Flint. It comes down the western side and flows into Lake Seminole in the southwestern corner of Georgia, where it also joins the Chattahoochee. The Flint River begins as an unassuming stream in College Park, a community close to the southwest edge of Atlanta. It never gets very far on its southerly career but it definitely becomes as river as it flows down through Georgia's lush foothill country on its way to Lake Seminole.

(Following page, above) Ducks enjoy a peaceful lagoon at St. Simon Island Club.
(Following page, below) Morning clouds cling to the Georgia mountains, near Dillard.

It touches towns like Albany and Bainbridge in its role as a commercial waterway, it flashes through the hill country around Warm Springs, drawing fishermen to its swift, muddy waters. It meanders along tree-lined banks in broad valleys, beckoning vacationers to come and play. Or it just looks scenic in its broad valley southwest of Macon, where it lends its own dimension to fertile orchard lands that produce the Georgia peach in such abundance.

The Chattahoochee River begins in the Blue Ridge of northern Georgia, touches Atlanta, brushes past Columbus, and joins the Flint in the southwest corner. It is long—436 miles—but not very wide or deep. Perhaps that has saved it from the intensive riverside development that might be expected with a stream that runs past Georgia's two biggest cities and is accessible along much of its length. There are giant lakes along its course where it has been dammed for power production and flood control. Much of the Chattahoochee, nevertheless, is in the shape it would have been without the help of man.

The name means "river of flowered stones," given to it by the Creek Indians, to whom the colored granite rocks in the bed represented underwater flowers. The river is regarded by some as a prime candidate for channel deepening, to provide clearance for bigger ships at Columbus and maybe even make a port out of Atlanta. On the other hand, conservationists have begun to lobby for its designation as a national recreation area, to preserve its scenic qualities. Some of the most beautiful stretches are in the Atlanta area northeast to Lake Lanier. The environment of the Chattahoochee is rich in animal life and a number of bird species are frequent visitors to its waters and bank sides.

The Coosa River is born at the city of Rome in Georgia's northwest corner. That statement is probably backwards. I should have said: Rome was born where the confluence of two rivers forms the Coosa. The Coosa is a Georgia river for only a little while. It leaves the state behind after only 30 miles and crosses into Alabama. Via the Alabama River the Coosa eventually reaches Mobile Bay, a distance of 587 miles. What is important for the city of Rome is that it could become an inland port were this large river system to be developed. Rome was once the Indian village of Chiaha, and its situation at the head of the Coosa made it a lively trading center then and later. Today's Rome is a big industrial town built on seven rolling hills (like its namesake) that rise up from the three rivers. So its setting combines utility and beauty. Some Romans see even fairer prospects for their city if the Coosa-Alabama rivers ever become navigable for heavy traffic all the way up to their doorstep.

(Preceding page) This waterfall on Tumalt Creek is one of many which draw lovers of natures to the Georgia countryside.

OKEFENOKEE, THE GRANDDADDY SWAMP

O kefenokee, as anybody who is the least bit interested in swamps knows, means "Trembling Earth." It is so named because where there *is* land that's apparently dry, it's frequently not very solid. Okefenokee is one of those now-rare places so primitive that its very nature finally defeated the efforts of man to turn it into something other than what it is. In 1889 the Suwanee Canal Company tried to drain it. The effort was a disaster. In 1908 a lumber company built a railroad into parts of it, on pilings, intending to log off its valuable cypress. Many trees in some areas of the swamp were indeed harvested, but the cost of the effort made the profits look decrepit. End of effort.

So the mighty and mysterious swamp has been breached and battered by some exploitative efforts, but has long since recovered from its mutilation. In 1937 President Franklin D. Roosevelt designated the area as a wildlife refuge. Today, 331,894 acres—about fourth-fifths of the swamp—are protected in all their primitive beauty as the Okefenokee National Wildlife Refuge, under the jurisdiction of the Fish and Wildlife Service.

Okefenokee has been around a long time. One educated surmise is that it probably began as a salt-water body that became separated from the ocean by the emergence of a reef on its eastern side (now called Trail Ridge). The surmisers also believe that Okefenokee started out looking more like the Florida Everglades than it does now. Being a much older formation, it has had time to build its "houses" of massed cypress and shrubs, islands that float on the dark swamp waters. It has been compared to the Dismal Swamp of Virginia-North Carolina, to Florida's Big Cypress, and to Big Thicket in Texas. But it is more varied than any of the others.

In the east are savannah-like open expanses—called "prairies" by the first settlers—choked with marsh grasses and water lilies. There is even some solid ground where pine-covered islands have become established. Western Okefenokee is more like a true swamp. It is heavily wooded with cypress bays whose thick covering provides shelter for the vegetation below. Even though some 400 million board feet

(Following page, above) Trees cling precariously to the rock ledges on the walls of Cloudland Canyon.
(Following page, below) Reflections enliven the still waters of this peaceful lake in Terrell County.

(Preceding page) A profusion of plant life flourishes in the watery stillness of Okefenokee.

(Opposite) Palm trees dot the sun-washed shoreline of Cumberland Island.

(Right) The historic State Capitol, with its golden dome, is a landmark in Atlanta.

(Below) The deep, still waters of Unicoi Lake reflect the changing colors of the deciduous forest on the distant bank.

(Following pages) Sunlight heightens the colors on the weirdly-eroded walls of Providence Canyon, near Columbus.

(Second following page, above) The Chattooga River flows through the Chattahoochee National Forest in Georgia.

(Below) Hungry gulls flock around a Georgia shrimp boat.

(Third following page) Amicalola Falls cascades down the rugged face of a cliff near Dahlonega.

(Preceding pages) Morning mists shroud Rabun Gap, near Dillard.

(Left) Rhododendrons bloom in the shady forests of Georgia.

(Below) The southern Appalachian Mountains roll into misty distances and deep valleys.

(Right) This shiner pond near Grand Bay provides nurture for innummerable varieties of aquatic plants.

(Opposite) Tempesta Falls cascades over a rocky escarpment in Tallulah Gorge.

(Right) Colorful flowers of many varieties thrive in Georgia's mild climate.

(Below) Winter's chill silences a mountain waterfall.

(Following page, above) Just outside of Atlanta, Sweet Water Creek runs through unspoiled Douglas County countryside.

(Following page, below) All kinds of greenery seem to thrive in the mild climate and fertile soil of the Georgia countryside.

(Second following page) Spectacular Toccoa Falls is near Tallulah Falls, northeast of Gainesville.

(Third following page) Clouds create a play of light and color in the Appalachian Mountains in northern Georgia.

of cypress were removed during the logging operations of the early 1900s, there are many monster trees of great age that remain.

In these dark forests legends and superstitions were nourished, first by the Seminole Indians who dwelt in the swamp and hunted there, then by a thin band of white settlers who eked out a precarious living on some of the larger islands. These big islands, numbering about 25, break up the brooding gloom of the dark swamp waterways. They support heavy growths of bay, oak, gum, and pine trees. The swamp forests harbor a variety of wild life, including otter, bobcat, white-tailed deer, black bear, rabbit, and even panther. Reptile residents number thousands of alligators, of course, but also turtles, frogs, lizards, and snakes of exceeding venom, like the cottonmouth, coral snake, and eastern diamondback rattler.

Okefenokee is valuable as a migratory bird refuge, and is becoming more so. Waterfowl and land birds winter here in increasing numbers. Mallards, canvasbacks, teal, and black ducks fly in to join the year-round populations. Herons and egrets come here, too. Then there are the birds whose antics and bright colors bring swift movement, melody and light: birds such as ruby-crowned kinglets, red-winged blackbirds, nuthatches and robins. Some of the common southern birds like blue jays, Carolina wrens, and crested flycatchers nest on the pine trees that grow on the islands. Red tailed hawks, bald eagles, and ospreys are seen there too.

Two small rivers, the Suwanee and St. Marys, drain the swamp, but the Okefenokee itself is a slow-moving river. Its northeast end is about 120 feet above sea level, and the swamp has a slight southwest slope. It begins south of Waycross in southeast Georgia and flows into northwest Florida for a few miles. It used to be only the very daring and adventurous who penetrated its ghostly waterways. Now tourists are routinely guided through it, on a regulated basis. But some of its secrets will always remain safe, as long as we hold to our resolve to protect is as a unique aspect of wild nature.

(Preceding page) Stone Mountain, a memorial to the heroes of the Confederacy, is a favorite attraction in Georgia.

WARM SPRINGS AND CALLAWAY GARDENS

Two exceptionally beautiful places in Georgia are closely related spiritually and geographically. Located within a few miles of each other in west-middle Georgia, they combine history and tradition with natural beauty. The places are Franklin D. Roosevelt's "Little White House" at Warm Springs and Callaway Gardens nearby. Both are in the Pine Mountain area and partake of the enchantment to be found in the soft beauty of the gently mountainous terrain.

The FDR "shrine," as it is sometimes called, does not convey that kind of meaning in any stuffy sense to the visitor who lets the full feeling of the place flood his consciousness. It is rather an opportunity for fond remembrance of a great man, in a lovely setting of piney woods, oaks, hickories, gums, magnolias and dogwoods. There is nothing pompous about the well-maintained grounds or the modest cottage that was built to FDR's specifications—and where he lived when he stayed at Warm Springs. As most people know, FDR was a gregarious man who disliked formality, and the displays of his personal mementoes in the Museum building on the grounds seem to emphasize this side of his nature. Even the 1938 hand-controlled Ford convertible that the crippled President personally drove around the Warm Springs area is on display in the garage.

The State of Georgia, represented by the Franklin D. Roosevelt Memorial Foundation, now owns and maintains the Little White House and more than 500 acres of adjacent land that was formerly the Roosevelt Farm. The stewardship of this important part of the national heritage by Georgia has been of the highest caliber, reflecting the perceptiveness and sensitivity of those engaged in this endeavor.

Callaway Gardens, like Warm Springs, is the legacy of a great spirit. Cason J. Callaway, who died in 1961, was a Georgia industrialist and a close friend of Roosevelt's. Like FDR, he was interested in improving the lot of his fellow man and,

(Following page, above) Golfing and boating are popular sports at Lake Sidney Lanier.
(Following page, below) Fernbank Forest, in Atlanta, is preserved largely in its natural state.

59

also like him, was engaged in experimental agriculture in the area for the purpose of improving farming practices there. One of his ambitions was to build the most beautiful garden possible as a permanent memorial to his mother, Ida Cason Callaway. In pursuit of this goal he conceived the plan for Callaway Gardens.

The Gardens' twelve man-made lakes are set off either by thick forestland or massed flowering shrubs and trees. In season, they flaunt their brilliant and subtle colors in a breathtaking display. At other times, when the leaves have fallen and the flowers are gone and the pine and hardwood forests are quiet, long vistas of woods and water open up to the visitor, and as he walks along a woodland hiking trail he is invaded by a sense of serenity and joy.

The Gardens are clothed in beauty regardless of the season, but the extensive greenhouses are especially rewarding to the winter visitor. While somber tones prevail outside and the air is frosty, inside the main conservatory spring bulbs are imparting a delicious perfume to the air. Massed displays of flowering bulbs delight and dazzle the eye. Through connecting doors a visitor may walk through greenhouses devoted to plants and flowers that grow within certain temperatures and climatic ranges. Even in the wintertime the floral show in these protected environments is a visual feast. For instance, a greenhouse for tropical plants grows exotic specimens from many parts of the world. The greenhouse complex is also an experimental area, with workshop components where new strains are developed both for display purposes and for the benefit of horticulture generally in west-middle Georgia.

A very pleasing touch in the Gardens is the small and exceptionally beautiful chapel, located at the end of a little lake in the midst of thick woods. The chapel's design is English Gothic, and except for the roof slates, it is built of materials native to Georgia. Several large stained glass windows flood the interior with soft colors on sunny days. The seclusion of the beautiful chapel puts the visitor into a mood of contemplation that adds an extra dimension to his visit to Callaway Gardens.

(Preceding page) Annie Ruby Falls breaks into several cascades on its way down the rugged cliff in Unicoi State Park.

THE NORTHLAND: BEAUTY AND BATTLEFIELDS

Atlanta, among its other roles, is by luck within hailing distance of Georgia's "Blue Ridge" country, a gateway to the beautiful, mountainous northland of the state. From west to east, north Georgia is a varied landscape of soft horizons filled with jumbled ridges and dense forests, big, lonely lakes, tall waterfalls, colorful and quaint little mountain towns, and mournful reminders of the past, from battlegrounds to Indian burial mounds. A wide swath of this countryside is within the protected confines of the Chattahoochee National Forest.

Georgia even has its own version of Arizona's Grand Canyon, at Cloudland Canyon State Park in the northwest corner, dubbed the "Little Grand Canyon." The park covers about 2,400 acres and contains some of the most spectacular scenery in the state. Sitton's Gulch, one of the area's rugged formations, is a sheer wall of gray sandstone cut by Bear Creek. It has scenic affinities with the big ditch in Arizona, and even a gorgeous waterfall that gushes from the side of the wall and plunges into the depths, its torrent delicately etched against the bulk of the yawning chasm.

(Georgia's Providence Canyon, far to the south, is probably better known. Providence is an octopus-shaped cavern with huge gullies extending from it, the central cavern covering more than 3,000 acres. A remarkable aspect of this canyon is its age—only about 100 years. The rapidity of erosion in this area is truly astounding, and the formation is undeniably beautiful—many colors make up the soil layers of its 200-foot walls.)

From Chattanooga to Atlanta, the Dixie Highway (U.S. 41) winds through this historic and scenic region, following Sherman's route closely. An important community on the route is Dalton, where the textile industry has made great gains in these last decades. Dalton is now known as the carpet capital of the world. It is also in the midst of rolling and mountainous terrain devoted to agricultural and dairy pursuits.

North Georgia was once the home of the Cherokee Nation and this region a center of their activity. The Cherokees were to lose their lands to whites avid for the

(Following page) The low-lying country around Brunswick contains many marshlands like these.

country's rich gold and mineral wealth. (The Gold Rush really began at Dahlonega, a little town about 75 miles to the east, instead of in California.) One of the reminders of their occupancy is found near Cartersville at the Etowah Indian Mounds, site of a former Indian village and burial ground. And one of the reminders of the more recent inhabitants is nearby: Alatoona Dam and Lake, one of Georgia's mammoth power projects.

Due east from Dalton, across the mountains and valleys of the Chattahoochee National Forest all the way to Georgia's eastern border, the lavish beauty pervades. The mountains shelter isolated communities where time has seemed to stand still, or at least to proceed at a slower pace than in most of the western world. The roads into the region wind around ridges in a succession of tortuous curves. This must discourage a lot of the hurry-up-and-get-there traffic and help to cut down contact with the world beyond the mountains. The people here hold fast to many of the traditions of their English forebears, keeping alive some of the old folk art, and even some Elizabethan flavor in their speech.

The southern end of the famed 2,050-mile Appalachian Trail begins on the summit of Georgia's Mount Oglethorpe. The hiking trail winds some 100 miles through the ''Bottom of the Blue Ridge'' before entering North Carolina. The mountains here live up to their name, with their deep, blue-violet coloration softened by an ambient haze. Some of the peaks raise their rounded crests 2,500 feet above the general 2,000-foot elevation. The dense forests covering the mountain slopes are mixed hardwoods and conifers, enlivened in the springtime by azalea and rhododendron, and all year round by the splashing of swift little mountain streams. Fall brings brilliant forest highlights as the oaks and maples turn red and gold.

One of the magical sights along the trail is Amocalola Falls, whose total drop of 729 feet is Georgia's highest. Near the state border the trail passes to the east of Brasstown Bald (4,784 feet), Georgia's highest mountain. Some of the best long views of lakes and broad mountain valleys in the state are available on hiking and riding trails out of Vogel State Park to Neels Gap and other points. Over on the eastern border is still-spectacular Tallulah Gorge. At one time, Tallulah Falls poured over a 1,000-foot precipice in a mighty torrent. Now Tallulah Falls Dam diverts a portion of the flow to a powerhouse, leaving the waterfall diminished but still impressive.

(Preceding page, above) Scarlet azalea basks in morning sunlight.
(Preceding page, below) The alligator, both an endangered and a dangerous species, is now protected by law in Georgia.

SAVANNAH

S avannah, a city that lives very much in its present, calls on its past to bring a dimension of living into today's world that very few American cities can count among their resources. Savannah is making a giant effort to preserve its original town plan, hundreds of historic buildings, and the general flavor and color of a city scaled to human beings instead of automobiles.

The preservationist movement began none too soon. That 20th-century dragon, the internal combustion engine, began to have its way in Savannah during recent decades. Spared by Sherman in 1864, the beautiful and functional city plan was in danger of falling instead to the private automobile and the commercial truck. But since the mid-1950s, many Savannahians have been rallying around their city squares and buildings, defending them from latter-day destroyers. (When General James Oglethorpe founded Georgia's first city in 1733, he designed those squares as defensive rallying points in another sense; today they are symbols of the accelerating effort to restore and preserve Savannah's heritage.)

General Oglethorpe envisioned Savannah, on its bluff above the river, as a series of wards each planned around an open square. Lots were reserved on the north and south of each ward for private homes, while ''trust'' lots flanking the squares on the east and west were reserved for the colony's public buildings. Oglethorpe laid out the first six squares before returning to England, and the plan was rigidly followed until 1855, adding up to 24 squares at that time.

Nearly all the squares are still there, beautiful pearl-like oases amid the traffic. And though many memorable structures have been lost to time or neglect, more than a thousand remain to tie the city to its past by lending their unique charm to the present.

As a result, Savannah is a city for strollers. On a Sunday—let's say in the early spring when the sun is warm and the flowers are in bloom—a walk south on Bull Street is a restorative to the body and spirit. Not only that, it's like a short course in Georgia history. The north end of Bull Street is on the river, where Factors' Row extends eastward on Bay Street, on the bluff above the waterfront. The old red brick buildings were once the offices of the cotton factors who were Savannah's movers and shakers during the 19th century. Today an exciting restoration is turning the old

(Following page) This peaceful country scene was captured in Cobb County on an autumn morning.

riverfront warehouses into boutiques, restaurants, taverns and galleries, making Factors' Row at once the oldest and newest of Savannah's attractions.

The Bull Street squares number five, and spread along the street's 30-block length to its southern terminus at Forsyth Park. The first square—and the first one laid out—is Johnson, named for the British governor of South Carolina, who was a friend of Oglethorpe's. It is embellished with stately live oaks, azaleas, and flagstone walkways. Then, like a history of Georgia, is scenic Wright Square; then Chippewa, its name celebrating the Battle of Chippewa, an American victory over the British in the War of 1812.

Next is Madison Square. One of Savannah's truly remarkable dwellings, in both a physical and an historic sense, is the Charles Green house, built in 1856 on the west side of the square. Its lavish gothic details bring some variety to the more austere architecture of the surrounding buildings. Now a church parish house, it was used by General Sherman as his Savannah headquarters during his occupation of the city. Green, a British citizen and Savannah merchant, had offered his residence to the general for this purpose. The facing of the house is stuccoed brick. It has Gothic Revival bay windows, intricate ironwork decorating its extensive verandah, and a crenelated roof. Inside are rooms of great charm with rich wood trim, fanciful moldings, and high ceilings.

Monterey Square, the last before Forsyth Park, was also one of the last to be laid out (in 1848). Being relatively new—from Savannah's perspective—it is not replete with old houses, though its 19th-century dwellings are interesting. In the center of the square is the Pulaski monument, honoring the Polish nobleman who was slain while helping the American forces trying to regain control of Savannah during the American Revolution. The beautifully-landscaped square is considered one of Savannah's loveliest residential areas.

The admirer of antiquity will want to explore the heritage left by architect William Jay. In 1817 Jay, a young (23) man of immense talent, arrived in Savannah, and over the next few years he designed many beautiful homes and buildings for the city. Several outstanding examples remain. The William Scarbrough house, completed in 1819, was the site of a reception for President James Monroe in May of that year. It was recently restored by the Historic Savannah Foundation and is now that group's headquarters. Another Jay-designed building which combines dignity with imaginative flair is the Alexander Telfair house, completed in 1820. It was willed to the City of Savannah in 1875 as a museum and now houses the Telfair Academy of Arts and Sciences.

(Preceding page) Flaming sunset reflects off the still waters of Billy's Lake, in Okefenokee.

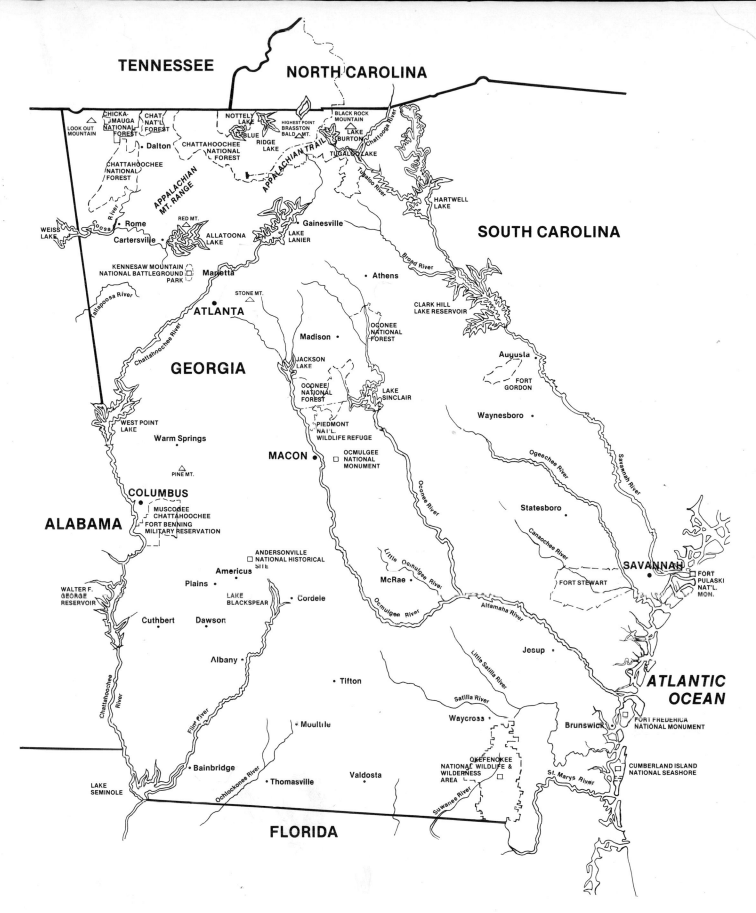

TENNESSEE

NORTH CAROLINA

SOUTH CAROLINA

LOOK OUT MOUNTAIN

CHICKA-MAUGA NATIONAL FOREST

CHAT NAT'L FOREST

NOTTELY LAKE

HIGHEST POINT BRASSTON BALD MT.

BLACK ROCK MOUNTAIN

• Dalton

CHATTAHOOCHEE NATIONAL FOREST

BLUE

LAKE BURTON

CHATTAHOOCHEE NATIONAL FOREST

RIDGE LAKE

TUGALOO LAKE

APPALACHIAN TRAIL

WEISS LAKE

Coosa River

• Rome

RED MT.

ALLATOONA LAKE

Cartersville

• Gainesville

LAKE LANIER

HARTWELL LAKE

APPALACHIAN MT. RANGE

Chattooga River

Tugaloo River

Broad River

KENNESAW MOUNTAIN NATIONAL BATTLEGROUND PARK

• Marietta

• Athens

CLARK HILL LAKE RESERVOIR

Tallapoosa River

ATLANTA

STONE MT.

Chattahoochee River

GEORGIA

Madison •

OCONEE NATIONAL FOREST

JACKSON LAKE

• Augusta

FORT GORDON

OCONEE NATIONAL FOREST

LAKE SINCLAIR

Waynesboro •

WEST POINT LAKE

Warm Springs •

PIEDMONT NAT'L. WILDLIFE REFUGE

Oconee River

Ogeechee River

Savannah River

ALABAMA

PINE MT.

COLUMBUS

MACON •

OCMULGEE NATIONAL MONUMENT

Statesboro •

MUSCOGEE CHATTAHOOCHEE FORT BENNING MILITARY RESERVATION

Canaochee River

ANDERSONVILLE NATIONAL HISTORICAL SITE

Little Ocmulgee River

SAVANNAH

FORT PULASKI NAT'L. MON.

Americus •

Plains •

LAKE BLACKSPEAR

Cordele •

McRae •

FORT STEWART

WALTER F. GEORGE RESERVOIR

Cuthbert •

Dawson •

Ocmulgee River

Altamaha River

Chattahoochee River

Albany •

Little Satilla River

Jesup •

Tifton •

ATLANTIC OCEAN

Flint River

Satilla River

• Moultrie

Waycross •

Brunswick •

FORT FREDERICA NATIONAL MONUMENT

LAKE SEMINOLE

• Bainbridge

Ochlockonee River

• Thomasville

Valdosta •

OKEFENOKEE NATIONAL WILDLIFE & WILDERNESS AREA

St. Marys River

CUMBERLAND ISLAND NATIONAL SEASHORE

Suwanee River

FLORIDA

(Following page) Blackeyed Susan brightens the verdant undergrowth in the Chattahoochee National Forest.